365

HEALTH &
FITNESS TIPS

365 Health & Fitness Tips

© Cover photographs: Adobe Image Library, Good Shoot, Photo Alto

Text: Dr. Magda Antonic
Translation: Beate Gorman
Copy editing: MediText, Stuttgart

Photographs: Adobe Image Library (19); Digital Stock (2); elektraVision (5); Good Shoot (3); John Foxx (1); MEV (14); Photo Alto (9); Photo Disc (8); Project Photos (1); Sertürner (1); Werner Waldmann (2)

© 2001 DuMont Buchverlag, Köln
(Dumont monte UK, London)

The advice given in this book has been subjected to careful consideration and examination by the author, the editors and the publishers; nevertheless, no guarantee can be given. No liability can be assumed by the author, the editors, the publishers or their agents for personal injury, material damage or financial loss.

ISBN 3-7701-7044-X
Printed in Slovenia

Contents

Spring

Spring is in the air. It is not very obvious yet, but the days are getting longer. The grey winter sky, the snow-covered fields and streets, the greyish brown colour of melting snow – many people begin to long for a friendlier, warmer and more colourful time of year. It's high time that spring came along! You now have something to look forward to. Nature will slowly but surely begin to change. The cold will make way for the pleasant warm air. And the first plants will begin to break through the hard ground.

1

Take some time to buy a few magazines. Relax in a café over a cappuccino and look at the new spring fashions. In your mind, slip into the new dresses, blouses and slacks. Will those shoes suit you? What do you think of the colours? There are sure to be some new makeup tips. Let your mind wander, and think about how you plan to give your appearance a new touch in the coming weeks.

2

Chafed, rough lips are unsightly and not particularly attractive. You can easily solve this problem by massaging your lips gently with a dry terry face cloth that has been placed for a few minutes on the radiator. In this way, you can remove the flaky skin and ensure that more blood is supplied to the tissue. Finally, apply a lip care product or simply rub some honey onto your lips.

3

Think positive: try to change the old ways of thinking with which you have apparently lived in harmony to the present day. If you are faced with a situation where your first thought is, "I can't do it", force yourself to say exactly the opposite: "I can. I'll try." Go about it with joy, curiosity, enthusiasm and eagerness and always say, "I can do that!" Use this technique even in banal day-to-day situations.

4

Relax by doing some eutonic exercises. This technique aims at creating a perfect balance between tension and relaxation. Lie flat on your back on top of a woollen blanket. Stretch your legs, keeping your heels slightly apart. Position your arms facing away from your body. Breathe slowly and intensively with your eyes closed. Remain in this position for ten minutes.

5

Eutonic exercises with your hips: Concentrate on your hips. With your skin, you can feel through your clothing the blanket on which you are lying. Concentrate on this skin contact and try to think consciously about the tension in your muscles. When you notice the tension, simply relax.

6

The seasonal change from cold to warm takes its toll on every fibre of our body. You now need regular doses of vitamin C, which works against the free radicals in your body. It doesn't have to be in the form of tablets or capsules: eat tropical fruit or press the juice from fresh lemons, grapefruits or oranges. Nowadays, water-soluble vitamin C does not have to be taken with meals; it can also be absorbed via the skin – several skin creams have effective vitamin C additives.

7

Soon you will be putting your polo neck jumper back in the wardrobe and showing more décolletage. Treat this part of your body to some refreshment. Mix about 1 fluid ounce of jojoba oil with $1/3$ ounce of carotene oil and rub this into your neck and décolletage. Then place a moist cotton cloth on top of this. Now place a terry cloth around your neck and the compress is complete. Lie down in a comfortable spot and relax. The neck compress should be removed after two hours.

8

Don't let spring tiredness get the better of you! A two-week nettle cure will rid your body of unnecessary ballast and put some life back into your metabolism. Pour boiling water over four teaspoons of dried nettle leaves and leave this to brew for around one minute. Drink the tea in small portions throughout the day.

9 Become more active and efficient by learning to walk properly. Straighten your shoulders, lean them slightly to the back and set off with your arms swinging (opposite arms and legs always swing synchronously), with your elbows bent at 90 degrees and your hands clenched to a fist. At the start, ten minutes are enough. Increase this gradually according to your own preferences. However, you should not walk for longer than an hour.

10 Make up your own walking plan. When you have had some practice, plan to walk four miles per hour. For a strong walker in good physical condition, this can soon develop into power walking: the target is five to six miles per hour.

11

Every now and again treat yourself to a power drink. Take a bunch of parsley and a bunch of dill, wash the herbs and chop them up. Mix them in a blender with a pre-cooled glass of yoghurt and a tablespoon of wheatgerm – a wonderful drink with plenty of valuable minerals.

Facial skin often becomes dry and scaly. This can of course be due to the wrong skin care or also to stress. However, in most cases it is simply caused by the effects of the cold weather. If your skin is dry and sensitive, stop using soap and cleansing agents containing alcohol and instead use fatty creams that have moisturising additives.

13

Every now and then take a cold shower.
Begin with your face. First let a thin trickle of water
run over your forehead, then over one side of
your face followed by the other side. Repeat this
facial shower four or five times. Next, move on
to your shoulders, back and chest – this will get
your circulation going again.

14

Do something for your grey cells and train your memory. It is important beforehand to structure all the information that you want to retain clearly and remember it in this structured form. Write down twelve objects on a piece of paper and look at it for two minutes. Cover the paper and then write down the contents of the first note on a second piece of paper. Your brain needs constant challenges – this is the only way it can maintain or increase its efficiency.

15

Are you feeling stressed out? Then do something about it and stop complaining. Take some time out and think about the tasks and situations that you find particularly stressful. Write down everything that you do in a day. Decide which of these tasks was unnecessary. Now use this to plan the following day. Learn to prioritise. Don't try to do everything at once. And also make sure that you do a few things that you really enjoy.

Oily skin – recognisable by large pores and a tendency to develop spots – requires a completely different type of treatment, namely a face lotion with an alcohol concentration of up to 40 percent. It can also be soap. Of course oily creams are not suitable. Use water-based face lotions or an oil-free gel instead.

17

Why not try some body balance exercises? For this, you need a special body balance ball, which weighs around five pounds. Exercise 1: Take a large step forward with your left leg, then lift the right heel. Hold the ball with your right hand with the top of your arm held tightly against your body. Now stretch and bend your upper arm five times. While doing this, bend and stretch your left leg. Then repeat this procedure with the other arm.

Exercise 2: Stand upright and in a straddle position. Let your shoulders hang down. Grab the ball with both hands and place your hands with the ball high above your head. Now bend and stretch your arms and legs five to ten times.

18

19

Exercise 3: Lie on your back and draw your legs in. Press the ball between your knees. Your arms should be at a slight angle behind your body. Now press the ball between your knees and release the pressure at regular intervals. Repeat this exercise ten times.

20

Exercise 4: You should again be lying on your back with your legs drawn against your body and the ball clamped between your knees. Place your arms beside your body at a slight upward angle. Lift your bottom a couple of inches from the floor, hold the tension for a few seconds and then let it touch the floor again. Repeat this ten times.

Exercise 5: Once more lie on the floor with your legs drawn towards your body. This time, stretch both arms out to the side. Hold the ball in one hand. Lift it from the floor slowly, hold it in the air and then let your arm drop to the floor again. Repeat this exercise five times for each arm.

21

22

Do something for your bust. A peeling will get rid of annoying spots and flaky skin cells. This can be done once or twice a week. Place the peeling mixture on moist skin and massage it in with a gentle circular motion. You will see how this stimulates the supply of blood to the tissue.

23

Take a handful of ice cubes and massage your décolleté and breasts. The cold makes the pores close immediately. If you have previously applied a skin lotion this works even better because it now remains in the skin due to the closed pores.

Give your connective tissue some spring power. Vitamin C helps to build up collagen fibres in the skin and improves elasticity. Provide your body with vitamin C by regularly eating fruit and vegetables, e.g. all types of berries, citrus fruit, cauliflower, Brussels sprouts, red and green peppers.

24

25

Outdoors, it is not really very warm yet. We are waiting for the spring. Still, there is nothing to stop you rejuvenating your body and soul. Take your partner and go dancing. Not in a disco, but somewhere where people do more than just push each other around in a sea of lights. Somewhere where you can dance the fox trot or a Viennese waltz. It is good fun and trains the body.

The ideal exercise for firm thighs: stand upright and spread your legs. With your back held straight, bend your knees and then straighten up again. If you are able to do this, you can lift your heels and stand on tiptoes. Place your hands flat against one another on your chest.

26

27

Many people long for a firm bottom; however, this does not just come on its own – you have to do something for it. Lie on the floor and pull your legs towards your chin. Place the heel of one foot on the opposite knee. Keep your hands flat on the floor. Now slowly lift your hips until the top of your body and your thigh almost form a straight line. Repeat this exercise several times.

28

This simple but effective exercise will give you great legs.
Stand straight with your legs slightly apart and your hands on your
hips. Stretch one leg to the side by putting your weight on the
other leg. Let your leg drop and repeat this exercise with your other leg.

29

Kneel on the floor and support yourself on your elbows. Make sure your back remains straight. Now tense your stomach muscles and lift one leg, keeping your knee bent. Hold your leg for a short time in the air then let it fall again. Repeat this with the other leg. Repeat the exercise five to ten times, alternating from one leg to the other.

30

Do you enjoy drinking coffee? You shouldn't overdo it. It is okay to drink up to six cups in the course of the day. But never forget to follow each cup of coffee with a glass of water! Coffee stimulates the kidneys to produce urine and if this liquid is not replaced, your body will dehydrate.

31

It is important that you drink enough! However, it does not always have to be expensive mineral water. In our part of the world, tap water is completely safe to drink. In this way you will save money and you don't have to carry all those heavy bottles from the supermarket. If you want your water to taste even better, buy a water filter. Filtered water is perfect and you know what you are drinking – which is not always the case with bottled water.

32

There are many reasons why the spring is a good time to lose weight; one of these is that slim people are less frequently annoyed by mosquitoes, which become active around this time. They prefer more corpulent people, since their blood tends to have higher cholesterine levels – a morsel for mosquitoes.

33

Why not try to stimulate your circulation with some simple acupressure: with the thumb and index finger of one hand, press gently against the little finger of your other hand for five minutes.

Some more acupressure to ward off cold hands: using your thumb and index finger, firmly press the point between the thumb and index finger at the back of your other hand for five minutes.

34

35

Do you smoke? Then you really should
ensure that you get enough vitamins;
one single cigarette destroys around 100 mg
of these substances vital to our health.

36

If you eat protein-rich food, you must remember to eat food containing vitamin B_6 often. Protein-rich food makes the body use up more vitamin B_6.

Fruit should ideally be eaten unpeeled,
as the skin contains the most vitamins.
Of course, you must take care to wash
the fruit thoroughly first!

If you have to stay awake for a long time, you should eat protein-rich food every three to four hours – but without fat.

38

Attack your problem zones! After a hot shower, massage your still moist skin with a firming body oil. Next wrap some cling film around yourself. Lie in a comfortable position, cover yourself with a warm blanket and enjoy the warmth for 30–40 minutes. This stimulates the circulation so that your skin will feel like silk afterwards. If you do this regularly, there will be no reason not to wear a bikini this summer.

39

40

Enjoy wonderful stimulating aromas: buy an aroma lamp, add a few drops of essential oils to the bowl and light a candle underneath it. Different oils give rise to different moods.

Aromatic smelling salts help release tension. The types most recommended are mixtures containing cedar or grapefruit oil.

42

Ylang ylang oil, the oil from the ylang tree, is an effective help against depression and inner tension. It is available at chemists' shops.

43

Massage yourself. To do this, all you need is a wooden massage roller. The surface of your skin should be dry. If you have showered or bathed beforehand, make sure to dry yourself thoroughly. At the start, just go over your skin lightly with the roller. When you feel that it is beginning to get pleasantly warm, increase the pressure.

44

If you massage yourself or your partner with a massage brush, always do this with circular movements towards the heart. Do not just stroke the body randomly!

45

You want to be thin – and without dieting? Buy
sea salt and add around 7 or 8 ounces of this to
your bathwater. Seawater draws fluid from the body
and purges it.

46

If you sleep long in the mornings, you burn off more fat. It is a known fact that the hormones that support the burning of fat are especially active during sleep.

In spring the weather can still be quite cool, especially in the morning. In spite of this, turn off the central heating and freeze for 15 minutes or so. Low temperatures stimulate the metabolism.

48

If you believe that your weight problems are simply caused by
your eating habits, try this recipe. Tell yourself several times each day
that you want to eat less and that you are looking forward to your
new figure. Write this down on little notes and leave these lying around
the house.

49

Calm your body from the feet upwards. A daily footbath relaxes tired feet and, if the right additives are used, it can have a similar effect on the whole body. Aromatic bath salts from the chemist's and a few drops of essential oil of your choice stimulate your sense of smell and have a beneficial effect via the skin. We recommend lavender or rose oil.

50

A tip which encourages you to give up certain habits but which
will have an amazing effect on your well-being: give up alcohol even if
you previously believed that wine, champagne or spirits put you in a
good mood. Alcohol makes you tired and bloats the body. And alcohol
is an absolute lust-killer in matters of the heart. Drink cool mineral
water and enjoy all the sensuality of this world completely sober.

51

Many people wish they had nerves of steel. It is a simple matter to eat your way to strong nerves: wholemeal foods such as dark bread, cornflakes, muesli and wholemeal cakes contain high levels of vitamin B. And this vitamin strengthens the nerves.

52

It is often difficult to stop thinking about food. Here is a little tip that may help you stop feeling ravenously hungry or at least get rid of cravings: Smell a bottle of rose or lavender oil, that you should always carry around with you. That quickly wards off the in-between hunger.

53

Do you have problems turning down that sumptuous looking dessert? If you spice up the main course with pepper or chilli sauce, you will probably find that you lose the taste for sweet things afterwards.

Chocolate doesn't make you fat – assuming that you do not eat bars and bars of the stuff. You can enjoy many things in small doses, even chocolate. One single piece before a meal even encourages digestion by stimulating the digestive juices – and that means that the subsequent meal is digested much quicker.

54

55

If your doctor has prescribed a diet or if you want to count the calories, you could even have an inner conflict when ordering a salad in a restaurant, because a dressing is used that will torpedo all your personal diet measures. Therefore, simply ask the waiter to bring the dressing separately, for example a yoghurt dressing.

56

Enjoying cup of coffee or an espresso after a meal is not a bad habit. On the contrary: caffeine stimulates the digestion process and trigonellin, an active ingredient in coffee, expedites the fat-burning process – something that is actually desirable after what may have been a rather filling meal. Of course, if you have problems getting to sleep at night, it is better not to have coffee in the evenings.

57

If you are worried that you will eat too much at dinner, try and fool your stomach: before sitting down at the table, drink a large cup of low-fat bouillon, preferably vegetable bouillon. Your stomach will be tricked and send signals to the brain that it is full.

58

Incense has been used for thousands of years. Apart from the fact that it disinfects the air, the balsamic aroma has a calming effect on the psyche. If you suffer from depression, incense can improve your mood.

Relax your scalp. First, comb in a hair pack and massage this substance into your scalp for ten minutes, using circular movements of your fingers.

59

60

When times are hectic, you should treat yourself to a herbal bath with fresh St. John's wort. Add three to four handfuls of St. John's wort to four pints of boiling water and allow this to simmer for half an hour. Strain the herbs from the water and add the liquor to the bathwater (temperature 98 °F). Do not remain in the water for more than quarter of an hour. After drying yourself, relax for an hour.

61

Why not try a cup of tea made with real camomile flowers? Buy a small pack of camomile flowers at the chemist's. The gently aromatic tea is not just effective in the treatment of colds and flu, it is also very good for stomach problems.

A honey bath will make your skin lovely and supple. It is easy to prepare this yourself. Mix five tablespoons of honey with eight drops of sandalwood and five drops of lemon oil. This mixture is added to a bath with a water temperature of 98 °F.

63

Cuddles as a therapy: nothing is more relaxing than having a cuddle, but don't postpone this until bedtime. Cuddling requires resolve and a certain amount of leisure time. You can also cuddle your dog or cat. The animals really enjoy it and for humans, stroking and caressing are great stress-killers.

64

If the weather outside is not particularly nice or if you do not really like walking in the city but feel the need for some movement, simply jog around inside your house! Put on some comfortable clothes and then off you go, jogging on the spot. Your steps become larger when you pull your knees higher. Swing your arms back and forth. You will soon work up a real sweat. A five-minute run on the spot will soon get your circulation going.

A lavender facemask after a bath is very refreshing. Add a few drops of lavender oil to a neutral cream (it is best to mix this with a mortar and pestle) and then apply the mask. Remove the mask after fifteen minutes and you will find that your face feels fresh and smooth.

65

Stretch your limbs. In bed, as soon as you wake up you automatically stretch your arms and legs. But during the day at the office you should take the time and stand on your tiptoes and stretch your arms as high as you can.

66

A cucumber facemask is very refreshing and stimulates the blood circulation. The mask is simple to make. You only need thin slices of cucumber, which you place all over your face; moist compresses are placed on top of this. Remove the mask after fifteen minutes and rinse your face thoroughly with lukewarm water.

67

68

When you arrive home after work you should not immediately attack the next household task. Relax for half an hour; mark the transition. Do absolutely nothing or make yourself a cup of coffee or tea. Stare into the air, breathe deeply and daydream. In this way, you will find new vitality for the rest of the day. If you spend all your time on the treadmill you become burned out, will often find yourself in a bad mood and run the risk of becoming ill.

69

Roses for your complexion: pour a cup of boiling water over a handful of fresh rose petals. The following day, sieve the liquid through a coffee filter and store it in a dark coloured bottle. When you want to prepare your rose mask, take around 3 to 4 ounces of the rose liquid and warm this with a teaspoonful of agar-agar (from the chemist's); stir this mixture until it becomes thick. Apply the warm paste to your face. After quarter of an hour, wash it off again with lukewarm water.

70

There is nothing to be said against the occasional sweet, but you will be doing your body a great favour (and improve your well-being and efficiency) if you limit your daily sugar consumption. For example, coffee and tea without sugar taste excellent. You just have to get used to the taste. Enjoy the natural flavour of food and drink. However, if you still have a craving for sweet things, it is better to use artificial sweetener.

71

Don't bottle up your aggression.
If you are angry at something or
someone, let off some steam. This
is important, and you will find that
it makes you feel better.

Music can have a very calming
and relaxing effect; however, this is
not true of every piece of music.
Buy a CD with music that helps you
daydream. You can also find music
that includes sounds from nature and
other recordings with nothing but
natural sounds. If you wish to get the
most benefits from such a CD,
withdraw to a quiet, peaceful corner
of your apartment.

72

If you have skin problems, one way to alleviate this is a tomato diet. For a whole week, eat and drink tomatoes in any form that you wish: raw, cooked, in soup, oven-baked or as juice. Tomatoes contain biotin (vitamin H), which is good for your skin and hair. Lycopene and carotene that are also contained in tomatoes are excellent antioxidants, which destroy the free radicals in your body (they attack cells).

73

74

Happy people live better and healthier. Happiness drives illness away or stops it taking hold in the first place. You can learn how to be happy. Simply turn a situation that makes you sad around, and don't take things too seriously.

75

White bread is not good for the intestines. Choose wholemeal bread instead. After all, there are no end of delicious varieties of bread available, from dark bread to toast. Some people don't like the taste of wholemeal bread. If you are one of these people, get rid of your prejudices and try some different kinds -- you will find that it is not hard to develop a taste for wholemeal bread.

76

Germinated seeds have a much greater concentration of valuable minerals, trace elements and vitamins than those that are not germinated. Therefore, buy mustard, alfalfa, mung or soybeans from your local health food shop.

Hygiene is very important. Even if you do not have too much time, never neglect your body. It is not just a matter of physical hygiene and cleanliness: caring for your body must become a ritual that is never postponed, but consitutes a highlight of your day-to-day life. No matter whether you shower, bathe or simply wash yourself at the basin, the important thing is that you carefully tend to all parts of your body.

78

A drink made from kombucha mushrooms helps solve many everyday illnesses, it regenerates the intestinal flora and is a good remedy for colds and flu. Kombucha can be bought as a tasty ready-made drink in a bottle, or the mushroom can be brewed up in tea with sugar.

79

You must nip anxiety attacks in the bud, otherwise anxiety will make you ill. Get a clear picture in your mind of exactly what causes these uneasy feelings. Then formulate a simple sentence – the command that these situations will not cause you to be anxious. For instance, if you are nervous about a job interview, tell yourself, "This interview poses no problem for me." Write this down ten times every single day and repeat it to yourself. Success is guaranteed!

Help your body to get rid of toxins and waste products. To do this, rub your body roughly with a dry brush, a sisal glove or a sisal belt each morning. Partners can rub each other. This is more fun and it makes the task easier.

80

81

As a bedtime drink, you should occasionally try a schnapps glass full of green wheat grass or barley juice. This takes some getting used to at first, but juices such as these get rid of toxins and stimulate cell growth. You could also dissolve a sprinkle of spirulina powder (river algae) in water and drink it.

82

Most people tend to wolf down their food. No one has any time and people talk and read over dinner – cardinal sins. Learn to chew properly again. Never swallow your food until you have chewed it at least ten times. Chew slowly and force yourself to count the chewing movements. In this way you will again learn to eat in a healthy manner. Besides this, eating will again become a pleasure. You only really taste what you are eating by chewing it intensively.

83

Calcium is an important substance for the bones. Turnip juice from organically grown vegetables is a good source of calcium. This is mixed with carrot and dandelion juice. But be careful when adding the dandelion juice – too much of it will make the drink too bitter.

84

If you press your own fruit and vegetable juices, add some nuts. They provide your body with extra magnesium. But be careful – nuts have a lot of calories, so if you want to lose weight, do not add too many.

85

Iodine is important for the thyroid gland. Buy wakame algae in your local health food store and pour warm water over it. Once this has cooled down, sieve it and add some to vegetable juice that you have pressed yourself or bought ready mixed.

86

Try the following recipe to fight dandruff and hair loss: boil two tablespoonfuls of allspice berries in a pint of water, let it simmer for 15 minutes and then let it brew for a further 15 minutes. Add some cider vinegar to the sieved solution. After washing your hair, rub some of this mixture into your scalp. Do not rinse this solution from your hair.

Summer

Nature is in full bloom and splenour, and there is not a single cloud in the deep blue sky. We feel the full heat of the sun, which is turning our skin a beautiful golden brown. Every now and then, a thunderstorm soaks the parched earth once more. We spend as much time as we can in the open air, seeking out the coolness of the forests, diving into swimming pools or lakes and romping in the sea.

87

Even if you are not yet able to enjoy the sea water because you have to put off taking a holiday, you can already grant your body this luxury right now: buy yourself some seaweed extract and take a sea bath in your very own bathtub.

88

If your body is lacking basic vital substances, it is in danger of overacidifying. This can lead to lack of concentration, depleted vitality and headaches. So remember: deacidify your body by absorbing additional basic vital substances, i.e. mineral substances and trace elements. You can of course achieve this by eating carefully chosen meals, but anyone who is short of time can also deacidify the body with special deacidifying agents from the chemist's. But make sure you still have a balanced diet and get plenty of exercise.

89

Insect bites can be very unpleasant. If you have been stung, you must first pull out the sting with a pair of tweezers. Add two or three drops of lemon oil to a teaspoon of honey and stir well; apply this mixture to the place where you were stung. You can also mix some more lemon vinegar with water and apply a cloth soaked in it to the reddened area of skin as a compress – this will lessen the pain and fight inflammation.

90

Sun-worshippers who have skin like porcelain should not venture into a swimming pool or go to the beach without sun protection, even if the sky is overcast. Whilst cloud cover reduces ultraviolet radiation by about 20 per cent, people with sensitive skin get sunburnt after only about 20–30 minutes without sunscreen. Apply your sunscreen about half an hour before sunbathing, because this is the amount of time required for the light protection filter to become effective.

91

Treat yourself to a rose bath: pluck the petals from two small roses and let the petals float on the surface of the water. A rose candle emanates a sensuous aroma. You can add five drops of rose oil to the bathtub.

Sunblocks with mineral light protection can protect against sun allergy, the symptoms of which are reddened skin and little spots. You can also start to take the sun protection vitamins A, C and E about a week before going on holiday. During the vacation, you should of course continue to take these tablets. After you have been sunbathing each time, you should soothe your skin while it is still hot from the sun, by using a moisturising cream – perhaps with aloe.

93

Help your body to produce its own sun protection factors. If you get a lot of exercise, a particularly large amount of oxygen reaches your blood via the lungs. This stimulates the formation of melanin, a sun protection factor in the skin produced within the body. And do not simply lie in the sun for hours straight away on the first day. Start with a quarter of an hour and increase your time on the beach by a further quarter of an hour each day.

94

This is how to get your cellulitis under control: with your knuckles, stroke the skin of your thighs from top to bottom and up again several times. Keep on doing this until the skin reddens.

This is another cellulitis exercise: place both hands on your thigh. Massage the tissue with circular movements of the fingertips. Do this for five minutes on each thigh. Then it is the turn of the insides of the thighs. Grasp the skin with your thumb and index finger and smooth out upwards.

96

Why not give your body a highly concentrated summer health treatment? On Sundays, eat strawberries to your heart's content all day long – as many as you like. They taste delicious and their calorie content is ridiculously low. A quarter of a pound of strawberries contain no more than 45 kilocalories.

97

People with so-called chocolate skin do not get sunburnt at all, no matter how long they lie in the sun. For them a sunscreen with a light protection factor of 8 to 16 is adequate. If you play sport in the sun, you should use a gel with photo-stable light protection filters. The effect lasts for several hours. After you have been to the beach, you should use Polynesian coconut oil (monoi oil) for moisture balance.

98

Collect stinging nettle roots. Crush them and put them into a tumbler with 40 per cent alcohol. All spirits are suitable for this purpose. Leave this mixture to draw for three to four weeks. Then strain it through a coffee filter into a dark-coloured bottle. If you are suffering from muscular tension or have a sprain, apply this tincture undiluted to the skin and put a bandage around it.

99

Use savoury from your garden as a bath additive for muscular tension. With an ounce of fresh flower shoots, prepare an infusion with boiling water, sieve it and add it to the bath water.

Lavender is well known for its relaxing effect. It is amazingly calming when used as a bath additive. Always be sure to mix lavender with other herbs, for example with rose oil, orange oil or sage oil.

100

Water is no protection against ultraviolet rays. On the contrary, the surface reflects these rays so that they have a much more intense effect on the skin. Particularly sensitive areas of the skin such as the nose, forehead, lips and the upper part of the body are at risk. The only help against this is a sunblock cream. By the way, as soon as you have left the water and dried yourself with your towel, you must reapply the sunscreen. By rubbing yourself dry, you also will have wiped off the sunscreen.

101

On Mondays, silicic acid is on the agenda. Millet is a good supplier of this substance, because it is the only grain that does not lead to overacidification in the body. The silicic acid contained in millet does your nails and hair a favour. You can boil millet and use it savoury or sweet as a side dish for any meal.

103

Tuesday is carrot day. You can extract the juice from the carrots and drink it chilled, or prepare salad or vegetables from boiled carrots. Why not cut yourself sticks to nibble on as well? Carrots contain carotin, which is converted into vitamin A in the intestine. Vitamin A reduces stress; it stimulates the immune system and is a boon for the eyes and skin.

On Wednesdays, purify your body with garlic. Garlic keeps the blood vessels clear, stimulates the blood circulation and supports the metabolism. Take a clove of garlic and add it finely chopped to bread thinly spread with margarine. Or concentrate it by making a salad with a lot of garlic. Those who do not like the taste or who have to mix with people the next day can also take garlic in the form of coated tablets from the chemist's.

105

On Thursdays, give your body generous doses of albumin and lecithin without burdening it with calories and cholesterol. Tofu is a secret recipe for keeping your veins free of blockages. This food is extracted from soy milk and can be purchased from any health food shop. Tofu tastes good in salads or as a side dish with soups and stews. There are also vegetarian sausages made from taste-concentrated tofu.

106

On Fridays, you enjoy the taste and the concentrated health effect of celery. The iron content in both stick and tuberous celery ensures that the blood is enriched with more red corpuscles. And more blood cells mean better transportation of oxygen in the body. You can eat celery as a vegetable or make it into a salad or a soup.

107

You should do something good for your tired legs. Put them up and place both hands around a thigh. Now massage the thigh from the top to the knee using slight pressure, and do this rapidly. When you get to the knee, let your hands go up again as they massage. Do the same with the lower leg – from the knee to the ankle and back again.

108

Get into the habit of waking up relaxed and alert in the morning! For this purpose, music is better than a shrill alarm. Then get into the embryonic position and roll out of bed that way.

109

Why not begin the day with deep breathing exercises at an open window? Oxygen is one of life's elixirs. Then comes the internal treatment: drink a glass of mineral water with a purifying capsule.

Even if the heat outside in the night is still oppressive and sleep just will not come, put your trust in the healing power of aromatic herbs. After letting some air into the bedroom, light a fragrance lamp with neroli, mandarin, lavender or marjoram. Applying several drops of essential oil along the spine is another tried and tested way of preparing for sleep.

111

You will find everything easier if you are in harmony with yourself. Believe it or not: you have to look after yourself first and foremost, discover your desires, and listen to your body. And do something for yourself. That is how you can achieve a harmonious balance – and you will be successful in whatever you do.

112

Do not always lie in bed in the one position. It is not good if the same groups of muscles remain under stress for hours on end.

113

Colours are life forces. The more intense the colours of fruit and vegetables, the more vital the substances contained within them.

114

Clean your teeth without chemicals one day – try a toothpaste with sea salt and seaweed.

115

Would you like a stimulant for your exciting evening for two? Add three teaspoons of freshly ground coriander to the contents of a bottle of red wine. It is better to choose a sweet rather than a dry wine. Seal the bottle and keep it in the refrigerator for a week. Sieve before drinking and bring the wine to room temperature.

116

If you have digestive problems, spice your meals now and then with chilli pods or chilli powder. But be careful when you do this. If you use dried chilli pods in your food, you should remove them before serving. If you have stomach pains, you must do without these hot spices.

117

If you suffer from circulatory insufficiency, it helps to add a generous pinch of cayenne pepper to a pot of freshly boiled herbal tea. Sweeten with some honey, stir well and drink this tea mixture regularly during the day. This will get you going again.

118

Bathing is an art. Before you leave the bathtub after a health bath, you should run hot water into it again for 30 seconds. Then when you come out of the bath, you can dispense with drying yourself off and you can wrap yourself up in your bathrobe straight away. The overheating of the last phase of your bath dilates your blood vessels and ensures that waste products are flushed out.

119

If you have trouble waking up in the morning, you can get yourself going by taking a shower. The temperature-change shower is also excellent training for the blood vessels: take a hot shower for five minutes, a cold shower for ten seconds, then have a hot shower again for three minutes. The effect is even more intense with a seaweed shower gel.

120

Treat yourself to a cool arm bath in the washbasin in between times – this revitalises the whole body.

Cayenne pepper works well against fever, for example if you have a cold. Boil a piece of peeled ginger root for three minutes in a pint of water. Add a pinch of cayenne pepper, half a teaspoon of honey and the juice of a lemon. Drink the liquid as hot as you can and then lie down in bed.

121

122

A cool shower at 68 to 73 °F not only provides relief if you are feeling edgy and nervous; it also cools you down in summer. But be careful: never have an ice-cold shower when your body is severely overheated. This could lead to a collapse of the circulatory system, even in healthy people.

When it is very hot, people like having ice-cold drinks. But this does not refresh them, because the body really needs cooling from outside – in the form of cold compresses or a cool bath. It is better not to have too cold a drink. Your stomach will thank you for it.

123

124

A paste made out of a cup of vegetable oil and half a spoon of cayenne pepper is helpful against bruises. On the first day after the injury, the affected area of skin is first cooled with ice. On the second day, you rub the paste on it and bandage it. Repeat this until the bruise has healed up. Of course, this recipe must not be used for open wounds!

125

Summer is the time for love. Prepare yourself an aphrodisiac of galangal root tea! Pour half a pint of boiling water over two level dessertspoons of chopped galangal root. Allow to draw for five minutes and then sieve the liquid. Enjoy a cup of this tea three times a day. You can also sweeten the drink with honey.

Diarrhoea is irksome, particularly when you are on holiday. Instead of taking medication, you will find that natural medicines, for example coriander buttermilk, can be a simple help. Add half a teaspoon of ground coriander fruit to a quarter of a pint of buttermilk. Mix well, and drink a cup of it two to three times a day.

126

127

Get yourself two plastic bottles and do fitness exercises with them. Jog on the spot. Take a full bottle in each hand with your elbows bent. Swing your arms backwards and forwards like this while you run on the spot.

128

With the bottles, it is not absolutely necessary to run on the spot. Take a step forward and swing your arms backwards and forwards. You can of course use dumb-bells instead of the bottles.

129

You can catch a cold even in summer! It mostly gets a bit cooler at night. So do not sleep without covers; use a thin sheet.

130

Drink colours! Pour still mineral water into a glass and place sheets of colourful cellulose film on top. In this way, you light up the water with the colour of your choice. Green is effective against nervousness, blue encourages sleep, yellow stimulates the digestion and orange improves your ability to concentrate.

131

If you have problems with your back when you are sitting down, you should buy yourself an exercise ball and use this instead of your armchair. It is not exactly easy to sit on a ball and concentrate on your work. This will not be a problem for you, though, once you have got used to it. In any case, it is much healthier sitting on the ball.

Do loosening up exercises now and again with your exercise ball as well. Relax and bounce up and down on the ball. You can also vary this and raise your arms alternately or at the same time.

133

Tip over while you are sitting on the ball
with your pelvis to the back so that the ball rolls
forwards with your bottom. Then your pelvis
is tipped forward and the ball rolls backwards
with your bottom. You can do these exercises
quite automatically now and then while you
work. This helps you maintain concentration.

134

Foehn wind can give you headaches and coriander tea helps to fight them. Grind two teaspoonfuls of coriander pods with a pestle and mortar. Bring the powder to the boil in a pint of water. After a quarter of an hour you can sieve the liquid. The tea can be sweetened with honey. Drink one to two cups in small sips as required.

135

An unforgettable summer night's party, until the early hours of the morning – how easy it is then to feel bad the next day because you have drunk too much alcohol. An infusion of galangal can help! Brew a teaspoon of crushed galangal with half a pint of hot water. Cover and leave to draw for ten minutes, and then sieve. Drink it in small sips.

Cardamom milk stabilises your metabolism and hormone balance! Crush some seed from a cardamom pod and mix this in a glass of warm milk. Sweeten with some honey. You should drink a glass of it each day.

136

137

Go out into nature and enjoy the radiant colours of summer. Light and colour will vastly improve your mental state.

138

How easy it is to sprain your ankle when you are hiking or playing ball! A ginger compress will then provide relief. Grate a fresh piece of ginger and pour hot water over it. When the liquid looks yellowish after a quarter of an hour, moisten a cotton cloth with it, wring it out and place it on your ankle. To keep it there, wrap a dry towel around it.

139

The skin often becomes inflamed after an insect bite. Turmeric oil helps to stop this. Mix a dessertspoon each of turmeric oil and almond oil, and apply this mixture to the affected area of skin. After half an hour, wipe the whole area with a cloth dipped in lukewarm water. You can repeat this treatment three to four times.

140

Nutmeg helps to combat digestive problems, lack of appetite, pains in the abdomen, diarrhoea or flatulence. Add a pinch of nutmeg to a herbal tea of your choice. You should drink a cup of it every day for one to two weeks at the most.

Air conditioning units are a relief when the weather is hot. But make sure that the devices do not blow directly at you. You can rapidly get hypothermia if they do.

141

142

Tick bites must be taken seriously! After a walk in the forest you should search your children thoroughly for ticks. Pay particular attention to the scalp.

143

Pull out ticks with tweezers. If the patch of skin becomes inflamed or fever or other symptoms arise, see your doctor straight away. Tick bites can cause highly dangerous infections.

144

If you like walking in the sun, be careful with perfume: if your skin is very sensitive, the perfume can permanently discolour the places to which it is applied.

145

A hot summer means sweating: the body loses a great deal of fluid, which you must then replace. It is best to drink water or tea, the latter unsweetened. Ready-to-use drinks with sugar do not quench thirst – the reverse is the case.

146

Do you have problems with athlete's foot? Crush turmeric with water to make a pulp and apply this paste to the sore fungus-affected areas. If this does not repel the fungus, you should see your doctor.

147

Summer time is holiday time. Do without alcohol completely while you are on board a plane. At high altitudes – with the resultant reduction in air pressure – the body has a much lower tolerance to alcohol than when you are the ground. Mineral water on the other hand keeps you fresh, so that you will be fit on reaching your destination.

148

Many people do not tolerate sitting for long hours on a plane very well because of their varicose veins. In any case, you should get up regularly and stretch your legs in the aisle or walk up and down on the spot. Support stockings hold back the blood from the legs and prevent health problems.

149

If you have done little or nothing as yet in the way of fitness training and if you always put this down to a lack of time, go to a good gym and take out a subscription. Once you have paid, you will want to keep to the schedule. This compulsion will definitely do you good.

Do not consider luxury to be unnecessary or mere affluence. Luxury is pure pleasure and everyone needs an experience of this kind to fortify his or her soul. So do not begrudge yourself something really special, perhaps even something utterly unnecessary and superfluous, at regular intervals. It should be pure joy for you – a wonderful treatment for your ego.

151

If you are keen to ensure that your bath
salts prove effective, you should always
undertake a whole body exfoliation before
the bath, as only in this way can the
skin also absorb all the active ingredients.

152

For a proper thyme bath, take two drops of essential thyme oil and five drops of geranic oil. This bath has a tonic effect.

Because of the lycopenes, tomato juice is one of the healthiest things you can imagine. Try a freshly squeezed tomato juice occasionally!

153

After a long hike, take an alkaline footbath. Add a dessertspoon of base salt to lukewarm water. Leave your feet in the water for half an hour. Then have a cold foot shower for a few seconds. Your sleep will be heavenly.

Using two ounces of dried Paraguay tea leaves, prepare an infusion for the bathtub. But do not have the bathwater too hot. This bath will take away your tiredness and gently regenerate your whole body.

156

Mechanical exfoliation is best carried out with almond meal. If you have very sensitive skin you must definitely exercise caution.

157

If you enjoy seaweed baths, don't get yourself just any seaweed. Make sure you only obtain products made from chemically pure algae.

Unripe tomatoes contain a great deal of solanine, and this substance can be fatal if you have too much of it. So be careful with unripe tomatoes!

158

159

Paraguay tea helps to stop headaches and it calms the nerves. However, you should not drink this tea with meals.

Autumn

There is a rather nostalgic feel to the last days of summer. It is gradually getting cooler, the foliage on the trees is starting to change colour and you can already foresee the splendour of autumn in a few weeks' time. Many people experience autumn as a rather sad time. The bubbly, exuberant life of summer, the time of outdoor parties and of rollicking around in the open-air swimming pool are at an end. You now often hide away at home, snuggle up on the sofa and enjoy a hot cup of tea. But autumn also gives you an opportunity for contemplation. Looking inwards, finding peace – that is the new challenge.

160

Give yourself a water treatment. Make a conscious effort to drink eight glasses of water at intervals throughout the day. Have the first glass after you get up – it is best if it is luke-warm. Before breakfast you can have your second glass cold. It is time for the third glass at some stage during the morning, and you can drink your fourth glass a quarter of an hour before lunch. Have glass number five after food but not during the meal. Drink some more glasses in the afternoon and before dinner; have your last glass before going to bed.

If you regularly drink plenty of mineral water, you will find after a few weeks that your skin has become much rosier and smoother.

161

162

Tired at work? Is the screen flickering in front of your eyes? Would you much prefer to postpone the stressful discussion with your boss? Just lean back, raise your shoulders and breathe in deeply at the same time. Then breathe out again straight away and let your shoulders drop. Repeat this exercise twice more. You will see that everything suddenly becomes easier for you.

163

If you do not have the opportunity to have a midday sleep because of your work, go walking in the fresh air during the break for about ten minutes – this will give you new strength and rid you of stress.

If you do not get much exercise and also do not have any desire to leave the house, get yourself a catalogue of fitness devices for home use. Perhaps this will make you feel like getting yourself a home trainer?

164

165

If you find the taste of your daily ration of water too boring, then you should boil up a small piece of ginger with your day's water requirements for five minutes. Then after cooling, pour the water into a pot. This is your ration for the day. In between times, you can of course also have a glass of fizzy mineral water for a change.

166

Those who get up early feel better all day long. The only thing is that you have to really get up! When the alarm rings, do not just turn to the side again and little by little fight your way into the day. After you wake up, have a really good stretch. Open the curtains, let in the daylight – or if it is still dark outside, switch on all the lights in the bedroom. Light ensures the immediate cutback of your body's melatonin, which helps you to sleep.

167

Get used to smiling a lot. Try now and then to make a conscious effort to smile to yourself – driving the car, going shopping, at work. Smiling will make you happy, and happy people find it easier to live and work.

168

You can also pull your face into a broad grin. Then pinch your cheeks. By this means, you can conjure up high spirits even if there is no occasion.

169

Are you too lazy to put on makeup every day? You do not have any time – but you would still like to look good? Try permanent makeup some time. A cosmetics specialist will use the finest needles to inject paint pigments into the skin so as to draw eyelid lines, eyebrows or lip contours. This makeup should last for up to five years.

170

Do not have any scruples about eating some chocolate now and then. This "sweet poison" is not harmful – in fact, the reverse is the case. It benefits the blood vessels and gives rise to hormones that promote happiness. You will only get fat if you stuff yourself with excessive amounts of chocolate.

171

Kiwi fruits taste delicious and are a fantastic provider of vitamin C. Have a kiwi fruit now and then as a snack between meals – this will make you fit for the flu season.

172

In a blender, mix the juice of two oranges, 6 to 7 fluid ounces of sauerkraut juice and 3 ounces of pineapple juice to make a real power drink.

173

A non-alcoholic drink made from a banana, a mango and 8 fluid ounces of carrot juice contains a lot of B vitamins and is highly effective against stress.

You can easily get digestive problems under control by adding bran or coarsely shredded linseed to your food.

174

Only eat pure yoghurt –
do not have it with fruit preparations, since they have
nothing to do with nature.
A spoonful of jam in natural
yoghurt tastes better than
fruit yoghurt from a test-tube.

175

176

Mix yourself a nightcap,
using a banana, an apricot, a
pint of soy milk and some
honey – you will sleep like a
log.

A bike ride, even in autumn, is more than just body training. It is a profound experience for body and soul. And it will be even more enjoyable if you ride with someone else or with a group.

177

178

A regular pattern of digestion is important for the whole organism. But this does not just happen on its own. The basic prerequisites for it are nutrition and exercise. And above all you should not ignore your body's needs.

179

Hopping is fun and it is healthy. You can hop on an exercise ball or even better on a trampoline. Hopping is beneficial for the body's musculature, especially that of the intestines. The rhythmical up-and-down movement relaxes the intestines and encourages digestion. If you regularly walk or run briskly, you will achieve the same effect.

180

Practise flexibility. Plan to get up 20 minutes earlier tomorrow morning and do breathing exercises at the open window.

181

If you master the technique of autogenous training, relaxation will no longer be a problem. Over the next few days, you should finally get around to enrolling yourself in a course.

182

This exercise is ideal for strengthening the trunk and abdominal muscles. Lie on your back and bend your legs. Raise your pelvis while leaving your shoulders on the floor. Then stretch a leg out straight ahead of you, return to the initial position and repeat this exercise with the other leg. Change over and do this a few times.

183

Try doing a few knee-bends after you get up each morning. Increase the number from day to day.

184

If you live in a multi-storey building, do without the lift one day and run up the stairs. This will get your blood circulation into top gear and will not take you any extra time.

Artichoke leaves are not just a delicacy, they also have concentrated healing powers. Artichoke preparations regenerate the liver, stimulate the bile flow and eliminate digestion problems. And you can thoroughly enjoy the bitter remedy in the form of a digestive liqueur, the celebrated Cynar – you do not even need to have a bad conscience!

Think of your heart and do not begrudge it vitamin C and cholesterol-lowering pectin. Mix yourself a heart drink out of half a pound of red grapes, an apple and an orange. Finally add another 3 or 4 fluid ounces of apple juice. A dash of lemon juice will make the mixture taste even more piquant.

187

Having a small glass of beer every day is like taking medicine. Centuries ago, Hildegard von Bingen considered beer to be a remedy – we know today that she was right in her judgement.

188

You will not benefit from the full effect of a health bath until your body is entirely immersed in the bath water.

189

Get yourself a wok. You really cannot prepare vegetables, meat and fish more healthily and more sparingly than in this round pan. The wok makes for short cooking times and gives more volume to your food.

Green tea provides you with important flavonoids, and apples give you pectin, a roughage material. Shred five medium-sized apples together with their skin into the blender and then add three cups of green tea (which must be cooled). Drink this strange-tasting shake thoroughly chilled.

190

191

When you use bath salts, be sure to check the water temperature. Get yourself a bath thermometer.

192

When bathing with essential oils, the water temperature should be between 97 and 104 °F. Baths with seaweed additives must not be hotter than 99 °F.

If you take a bath with seaweed extract, you should not wash yourself off under the shower or rub yourself down with a towel, because the algae should continue to have an effect on the body.

193

194

If you collect your own medicinal herbs, you should not pick them from beside the road because of the hazardous substances. Nor should you use them immediately after they have been fertilised.

195

Treat yourself to a drink that puts you in a good mood, tastes wonderful and stimulates the brain: shred half a watermelon and honeydew melon and place in the blender. Then pour in some freshly grated ginger and two teaspoons of honey, some lemon juice and two cups of mineral water. Serve this stimulating drink cold.

During pregnancy, you have to be careful even with natural remedies. The following essential oils, for example, must not be used: angelica, aniseed, basil, tarragon, fennel, laurel, peppermint, rosemary and juniper.

196

197

The health-giving effect of ginkgo is not just beneficial if you consume this substance – in cosmetics, too, ginkgo has an effect on the entire organism. If you want to put this knowledge to use, buy yourself shampoo and hair lotion containing ginkgo. In creams and lotions, ginkgo stimulates the blood circulation under the skin.

Your memory likes to be trained regularly. Buy yourself a book with memory-training exercises.

198

199

Make sure your cosmetics do not contain any hazardous preservatives.

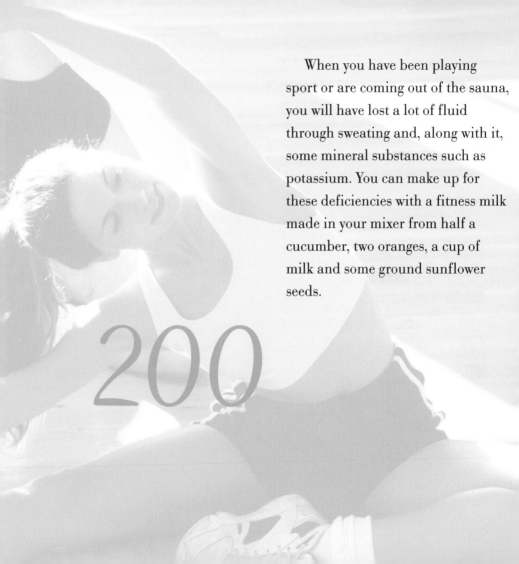

When you have been playing sport or are coming out of the sauna, you will have lost a lot of fluid through sweating and, along with it, some mineral substances such as potassium. You can make up for these deficiencies with a fitness milk made in your mixer from half a cucumber, two oranges, a cup of milk and some ground sunflower seeds.

200

This soy shake, rich in selenium, potassium and vitamin C, will give you roughage en masse. Into the blender put a banana, $3^1/_2$ ounces of strawberries, 8 fluid ounces of soy milk, two dessertspoons of barley flakes and a teaspoon of honey to sweeten. After mixing, leave the shake to stand for five minutes so that the barley flakes can continue to swell.

201

202

Essential oils are not water-soluble, so you have to dilute them beforehand in a solvent. This can be done with milk powder, fresh egg yolk, sweetened cream or special dispersion preparations from the pharmacy. Without this dilution, small droplets of oil would float on the surface of the water and could do damage if they were to get into your eyes.

203

Essential oils such as sage, rosemary or thyme can raise your blood pressure, so they are unsuitable for people whose blood pressure is already high.

204

When you buy essential oils, make sure they are of impeccable quality. Synthetic oils are not suitable. Price is an indicator of quality: good essential oils simply cannot be cheap.

205

Muscular pain after exercise can be treated with a carrot
melon shake containing a lot of potassium. In a mixer,
make a honeydew melon into a shake with 8 fluid ounces of
carrot juice. To refine the taste you can add lemon juice
or a spoonful of natural yoghurt.

206

The following mixture of fragrances makes a good start to the day: put one to two drops each of carnation, rose and blood orange oil in some warm water and pour this mixture into the perfume bowl.

207

Do not baulk at a low in performance that suddenly occurs during the day, and do not begrudge yourself a necessary break. Our rhythm is determined by our "internal clock".

Try pumpkin seed oil some time when you are dressing a salad. It contains large amounts of vitamin E (good for libido!) and it lowers the cholesterol level.

A few hazelnuts that you chew thoroughly and insalivate before swallowing are a good remedy for heartburn.

209

210

This vital shake rich in magnesium is not just a boon for women over 40 and a good preventive against osteoporosis: two kiwi fruits, two bananas, a papaya and an orange are pureed in the blender with a cup of milk, some natural yoghurt and a pinch of vanilla sugar.

211

Here is a healthy tip when you are feeling a bit peckish in between times. Keep your fingers off the snacks that are advertised on TV; instead nibble a few nuts, a muesli bar containing a lot of roughage, eat a natural yoghurt or just have a piece of fresh fruit.

212

To give your digestion a helping hand, you should try this drink containing a lot of roughage: in the blender, puree a jar of sour cherries, two dessertspoons each of rolled oats and ground hazelnuts and half a banana. Finally add a cup of full-cream milk and a tub of natural yoghurt.

213

Buy yourself these essential oils: lavender, marjoram, juniper and fennel. This blend of oils causes a scent to enamate from the fragrance lamp that will thoroughly and deeply relax you.

A fragrance-oil mixture made from lavender oil, nutmeg oil and lemon balm oil is an ideal way of finishing off the day and it will give you pleasant dreams.

214

215

Those who know themselves really well prefer to resolve or avoid conflicts that can make them physically ill. A good path to your inner self is to regularly confide your thoughts to a diary. There you can put absolutely everything down on paper that is going through your mind. In autumn in particular, you tend to become more contemplative. Later, when you read again what you have written, lots of things will be more comprehensible to you.

216

Take the time to write down which moments in your life have been particularly happy. Draw up a real happiness list. And one day when you are feeling down, fish out this piece of paper and read it. With the remembrance, those positive feelings will again take possession of you.

217

Drink green tea. Get yourself a good book from which you can learn everything about this wonder drug. Green tea is more than just a drink – it is a philosophy.

Green tea also makes you beautiful. Dip cosmetic pads in cold green tea and put them on your face as compresses; leave them in place for a quarter of an hour.

218

This immune-strengthening apple shake is irresistable by reason of its unusual taste combined with garlic. Put two to three apples, an orange, and – to add to the taste – a cup of apple juice and a teaspoon of honey in the blender. Crush a clove of garlic in the garlic press and add it at the end.

219

220

Alcohol is not the only appetite stimulant. There are healthier variations, like this tomato paprika aperitif: mix together two glasses of tomato juice, a glass of artichoke juice and a glass of paprika juice. It is best to prepare the juices freshly. Add to this a dash of Tabasco sauce, a pinch of chilli and nutmeg and fresh basil leaves. Served cold, this appetiser really gets you going.

221

Aloe vera contains 160 skin-active substances and in this way it supplies the skin with all the necessary vitamins, enzymes and amino acids. In case of sunburn or other skin irritations or for sensitive skin in general, aloe vera juice is considered to be the number one remedy. At the cosmetics shop, ask for products with aloe vera.

222

One day, have a good think about your feelings. What is it that upsets you again and again? You could talk about this with friends or keep a diary. Perhaps your reactions are sometimes exaggerated; lack of detachment very quickly leads to stress. So clarify what points in your emotional life are feeling sore and try to dispense with a little stress in future.

223

In autumn, the weather gradually becomes colder, and so digestion also becomes more sluggish. Aromatic cardamom not only awakens all the vital spirits, it also encourages digestion. Drink black tea, to which you add two to three cardamom seed pods before brewing.

If your adrenalin level is rising because you are getting worked up, put on your jacket and go outside. Do a round of jogging, and as you do so, think about nothing at all – just concentrate on your body and your breathing. You will be amazed at how quickly you can shake off your anger which would otherwise keep gnawing away at you.

225

Seaweed products give your hair new strength: the algae particles are absorbed by the hair when a hair pack is used; in this way they work in intensively. The hair becomes stronger and more voluminous.

226

Eat garlic regularly. You can add garlic to practically any food, and now and then you can also just chew a clove of garlic by itself. Drink a glass of milk to alleviate the pungent aroma.

227

If a plan goes wrong, do not continually be at odds with it – just let go. Consider an alternative. Perhaps you have been wanting to read a particular book for a long time: if your visit to the opera performance has fallen through again, simply take the opportunity to do something different.

228

Balanced nutrition should be fun and should give you a positive feeling about life. People who feed themselves on a bad conscience are burdening their mental balance. So do not be too strict with yourself and occasionally consciously ignore your little nutritional sins. In this way, you can even thoroughly enjoy a hamburger or fatty potato crisps.

Raw fruit and vegetables are a blessing for the digestion, but do not have too much of a good thing. If you change over to raw fruit and vegetables from one day to the next and your digestive apparatus is not used to this, you will have problems. Raw fruit and vegetables – particularly if they are consumed in the evening – stay in the intestines overnight and ferment. This leads to abdominal pains and flatulence. So break in your consumption of raw fruit and vegetables gently.

229

Saffron is very expensive, but you only need a very small amount of it for a meal. Saffron promotes the digestion and is considered to be a remedy for depression. But be very careful with the dosage.

230

231

There can be no objection to a small glass of aniseed brandy if you drink it at the end of a sumptuous meal to aid digestion.

232

Do you like to brood over things? Do you sometimes become endlessly fixed on a problem? When you go to bed, you should switch off. Simply snap your problem shut as you would a book. Often your subconscious will present you with a solution the next morning.

233

Monks have known about this for a long time: consuming figs gets the intestines going. Just eat one to three fresh figs before going to sleep each evening. There is no better-tasting laxative.

In the history of natural healing substances, incense is considered to be an agent that promotes blood circulation and disinfects. If you suffer from inflammation of the mouth and throat, you can paint the inflamed mucous membrane spots with a tincture of incense. Your pharmacist will prepare the tincture for you.

234

235

Do you get tired quickly and suffer from low blood pressure? Rosemary can remedy this gently and safely. Pour half a pint of hot water over a teaspoon of dried rosemary leaves and leave this tea to draw for a quarter of an hour before straining. However, you should not use this remedy during pregnancy.

Milk can be used in external applications, too. Lactic acid gets rid of bacteria, and proteins give the skin new power. Ask your beautician for special care products made from milk or whey.

236

237

When did you last do something wonderful with someone you love? Maybe a walk in the autumn forest or an evening meal at your favourite restaurant. Do it today and have a great time.

If you change your diet, do it in small stages because otherwise you will not discover the true pleasure of the new diet and will soon get back into your old habits again.

238

239

Do not trust any diets that promise miracles. In the long term, they are almost always completely ineffective, whilst the nutritional deficiencies can damage your health.

240

Do not get annoyed if, for instance, you have to wait in a long queue. Your annoyance will not get you one step further; it will just sap your mental and physical energies. Be grateful for the opportunity to have a few minutes of time for your thoughts – just imagine how you would like to organise your leisure time or your forthcoming holiday.

241

If you are angry with a colleague who has given you a lot of trouble, do not get too steamed up; instead, you should regard the matter as an opportunity to have a good think about what has caused these problems. Your body will thank you for keeping calm and collected.

Press-ups are an ideal workout for the whole body if you do them consistently and regularly. Make sure that your back is as straight as an arrow from your bottom to the top of your head.

242

Go for a walk in the forest. Shuffle through the colourful autumn foliage, and delight in the colourful splendour of nature. Stop now and then and fill your lungs with the fragrant air.

243

244

Cook more tastily and more healthily! Do without excessive amounts of salt and pepper and trust more in the taste of the food itself. There are many spices that give a whole new accent to a dish and that also have a beneficial effect on health. Why not try freshly chopped parsley, oregano, dill, aniseed and caraway seed?

All exercise is beneficial to the body, even rollerblading. If you indulge in hazardous sports, you simply must make use of all recommended safety measures so as to protect yourself from injury.

245

Learn the technique of meditation. For the approaching long evenings of winter, this would be a good opportunity to accept your body and become aware of its problems. Television simply whitewashes everything and continues to leave your mind weighed down and burdened. You can learn meditation through courses or at a monastery or convent.

246

The problem of strong-smelling breath after eating garlic can be remedied by chewing fresh parsley, a coffee bean or green tea leaves.

247

248

If you suffer frequently from heartburn, you should take these rules to heart: instead of eating a lot, it is better to have several meals at intervals throughout the day. Fatty food is taboo. You must chew everything thoroughly. Avoid cigarettes and alcohol. Do not wear tight-fitting clothes. If the heartburn persists, you should see your doctor.

249

People who do not like meat have to obtain protein from other food sources (low-fat milk products like curd cheese, yoghurt and cheese or eggs, potatoes and fish). If you are not a strict vegetarian, you should include a small portion of meat in your menu now and then in the interests of a balanced nutrition. Meat is particularly important for the nutrition of children.

250

If you have decided to do something regularly for your health at a gym, you should have a close look at the institution of your choice. It is important – before and during training – that you receive advice and supervision from an expert. Before you start training, you should be examined by a sports doctor.

Diabetes is a widespread illness which is primarily a result of our modern way of life and a lack of sensible nutrition. At least once a year, ask a pharmacist to measure your blood sugar. Otherwise, you will not notice that you have diabetes until the disease is far advanced and has possibly already caused damage.

Always carry a few cloves
in your pocket and chew one
instead of the usual chewing
gum. This will get rid of
bad breath and calm your
stomach.

252

253

If you eat a lot of meat,
you should season side dishes
such as potatoes thoroughly with
marjoram, because this herb
is effective against fermentation
processes in the intestines.

You can jog and run at the cold time of year, too. In rainy weather you should wear shoes made of waterproof, breathable Gore-Tex. The clothing must absorb perspiration and still feel dry. Cotton is not recommended; textiles made from micro-fibres are better.

254

With a massage band, you
can treat your back by pulling the
band to and fro behind you.

255

256

Electric foot massage devices
can be bought in department stores
and specialist outlets – you place
your feet on the vibrating top of these
devices. This treatment is very
pleasant and is effective in stimulating
blood circulation.

257

Cinnamon stimulates the digestion and is a proven remedy for flatulence. It also encourages a stronger circulation and raises the blood pressure if it is too low. So use more cinnamon in seasoning your meals.

If you are annoyed with someone
to such an extent that it is almost
making you sick, write an open letter.
Get everything off your chest. But
do not send this letter. You will
be surprised at how much better you
feel.

You and your partner should massage each other. But in so doing, take heed of a few rules. Never massage the bones; stop when it hurts; and you should loosen yourself up beforehand by stretching or by doing circling movements of the head.

259

260

The following vegetable oils are suitable for a massage: almond oil, grapeseed oil, soy oil, wheatgerm oil, avocado oil, apricot seed oil, cherry seed oil, carrot oil, jojoba oil. Olive oil too can be used if you do not mind the smell of salad dressing. But for the massage you should use the oil sparingly.

Cardamom used regularly as a seasoning has a general detoxifying effect on the whole body.

261

262

If you suffer from heartburn from time to time and are overweight, you should seriously consider losing weight consistently. Obesity often contributes to heartburn.

263

In many medicinal baths or
saunas, there are also special pools
for treading water. This activity
is fun and combines the pleasure
of cool water with exercise.

264

Dry-brushing does not just give you a pleasant feeling, it also supports the work of the internal organs. By gently circling with a dry brush over the stomach, you stimulate the intestines – a good remedy against digestive complaints.

265

Chilli is not just a spice to make foods hot. It also has a unique
health-giving effect. The capsaicin contained in the chilli dilates
the blood vessels, thins the blood (a good preventive against heart attack
and apoplexy) and stimulates the production of digestive juices. You
can use chillies to season practically any dish.

266

Ginger is an important remedy in Chinese medicine. Its positive effects in curing lack of appetite and nausea cannot be disputed. Ginger contains ginerol, which is similar in its chemical structure to the active ingredient contained in aspirin and therefore has a blood-thinning effect, i.e. it can protect against heart attack.

If you are constipated, you should not take laxatives but rather you should promote regular digestion by supplying your body with roughage.

267

268

Not all yoghurt is beneficial to health. Valuable lactic acid bacteria are destroyed by heating, so do not buy yoghurt that has undergone heat treatment.

269

Lavender oil is one of the most popular oils for massage, because it has a calming, relaxing, anti-inflammatory and pain-relieving effect.

270

A healing effect has even been attributed to magnets. The healing effect of magnetic field therapy using special devices has been scientifically proven. Non-medical practitioners use them, but you can also buy them yourself.

271

There are plenty of overweight people who would like to get their weight down by making an effort for a couple of days to eat as little as possible or nothing at all. This does not work, because afterwards you are even more ravenously hungry and you end up putting on weight. Try to eat a balanced diet – you will do better in the long term.

272

For mild headaches, stroke the tension evenly out of your forehead with the backs of your hands. You can also use your fingers to stroke outwards from the middle of the forehead with moderate pressure.

273

A foot massage has a positive effect on the whole body, as there are many nerve ends in the feet. Stroke with your thumb from the heel to the roots of the toes.

274

Boil rice in water with a pinch of salt to make a soup. For three days, consume nothing but this rice water. This will free the body of metabolic toxins.

Eat a medium-sized raw or steamed onion now and then. This will ensure that sufficient lactic acid bacteria are formed in the intestines.

275

Winter

When we think of winter, we generally conjure up images of a dreamy snowy landscape, smell the powdery snow as we ski and hear the crunching sound of boots in the snow. But reality is often quite different: cold, rain, snow and slush make our nose run and force us into bed with a fever. The cold season presents a major challenge to the immune system. But we can easily get the upper hand.

276

Let your immune system run at full speed. Get yourself a diet consisting of a good 50 to 60 percent carbohydrates, 30 percent fats and 10 percent protein. In other words, your diet should be largely vegetarian. Meat, sausages, milk and dairy products should play a greatly reduced role in your nutrition; but eat fish regularly.

Vitamins, mineral substances and trace elements are mainly found in fresh fruit and vegetables. You should get used to eating five portions of fresh fruit and vegetables a day, so that your body is not lacking in any of these important substances. And remember that tinned vegetables – as opposed to frozen food – are lacking a lot of these substances. Many vitamins are also destroyed during cooking.

278

If you include one or two cloves of garlic in your diet every day, you reduce the risk of developing an infection. Garlic encourages the circulation of the mucous membranes and strengthens them against infections. Instead of using salt, you can also season your meals with garlic. But if you are afraid of the unpleasant smell after eating garlic, you can also take it in the form of capsules.

279

Rose hip tea is rich in vitamin C. So now and then choose to do without your beloved glass of wine or beer and drink rose hip tea instead. You can obtain the vitamin-rich tea in practical tea bags. Or you can of course make it yourself by gathering dog roses.

280

Make a conscious effort on these dark, cold days to eat more carbohydrates. Half your daily diet should consist of bread, grain, potatoes, noodles, rice and rolled oats. This will reduce your appetite for longer and provide your body with more energy to well and truly brighten up even a dull day.

Do not believe the fairytale about winter flab. People who live in a particularly cold region – in the Antarctic maybe – certainly need a large amount of winter blubber because the body burns such fat and converts it into heat energy. For anyone living in the more temperate zones, no more than 30 percent fat should be supplied to the organism in the daily diet. And if you really must use fat, then use unsaturated fatty acids such as seed or olive oil. Avoid butter and bacon, even if they taste good.

282

Living it up really means placing a strain on the body. In summer, things are not so bad since we inevitably stay outdoors a lot and get sufficient exercise. In winter, however, we certainly prefer to sit around indoors. So you should eat wisely, avoid heavy meals and also not be too generous with the alcohol.

283

Horseradish contains essential oils that disinfect the mucous membranes and thus ward off bacterial attacks. But they also keep the airways really well ventilated. Buy yourself a piece of fresh horseradish and grate a small heap of it. It tastes great with a meal, and you can also use it to prepare a soup or curd cheese.

284

The changeover between hot room air and moist cold air outside is tremendously taxing on the skin, which then becomes rough and dries out. In any case, people who suffer from dry skin should use a skin cream with oil and regularly apply it to their face.

285

Change your perspective in bed! Get yourself two blocks of wood
of equal size and use them to raise your bed at the head end. When you
come home from work, put on light clothing and lie down on the bed
with your face downwards. Close your eyes and listen to the depths
of your soul. Let your thoughts wander. Dream away to yourself. You
will relax wonderfully, and the evening is yours!

286

Immediately after you get up, try to fill up with energy for the day in the space of three minutes. The secret is nothing spectacular: with both hands, grasp your wrists and hold them firmly. Then press both arms apart with all your strength and tug at your wrists. Try to maintain this tension for ten to 20 seconds and then drop your arms.

287

Are you facing an examination or working overtime? To strengthen your nerves and increase your ability to concentrate, eat walnuts.

288

Influenza is no joy. If you have become infected, you should trust in the strength of your immune system. For weakened or elderly people, flu can be life-threatening; timely flu injections are highly recommended for this group of people.

Is winter a time to refrain from bathing? Not at all! You can bathe at home. With all kinds of bath salts, you can create enjoyment, a sense of well-being and health. For stress and nervousness, bath salts with valerian, lavender, balm, orange blossom, hayseed or juniper are recommended.

289

290

If you are feeling worn-out and tired but simply do not want to lie down and sleep, have a pine-needle bath – or take rosemary or eucalyptus bath salts. These medicinal herbs stimulate blood circulation and will cheer you up.

291

Take cold prevention measures. If you take plant substances that stimulate the body's own immune system in good time, you can confidently venture onto buses and trains full of sniffling people.

Echinacea preparations in drop or tablet form strengthen your immune defences over the critical period. But if you already have a tickle in your nose, you should take the preparation every two hours.

292

293

The skin protects itself with a hydrolipidic film. The harmful substances from the environment are deposited on the skin every day and block up the pores. But if you have hot showers with soap and lotion too frequently, you not only take the dirt out of the skin, you also destroy its natural protective film. So be careful to use water sparingly and apply cream straight after you shower or bathe.

Correct breathing has to be learned – even if you find this difficult to believe. Most people breathe too shallowly, too unconsciously. First learn what it really means to breathe. Lie down comfortably and flat on the floor and allow all the air to slowly escape from your lungs. Then breathe quite deeply through your nose again. Pay attention to this process and feel how your lungs fill with air. Repeat this exercise about ten times without haste.

Begin the day quite consciously with a wonderful breakfast even if you are accustomed to gobbling down your breakfast in the morning in a hurry. Get up extra early and give yourself time. Enjoy fruit muesli, a steaming cup of coffee or tea and a coarse wholemeal bread roll with margarine and honey. To finish you might like an apple as well – take your time peeling it. Avoid all hustle and bustle. Do not think about your schedule for the day. Instead, spend ten minutes reading the newspaper.

295

296

It gets dark earlier at this time of year. So your trip home early in the evening is already turning into a tiring night journey. Do something to please your eyes and do not begrudge yourself the regular doses of vitamin A present in carrots, milk and cheese. Particularly helpful and tasty is freshly squeezed carrot juice – but you must add a drop of oil, because only in this way can the body utilize the vitamin.

If you take vitamin E tablets to reduce the ageing of cells, to increase the body's oxygen utilization and also to give you greater sex drive – not a bad idea for long winter evenings – you should make sure that you do not eat vegetables rich in iron (like spinach) for a few hours after you take your tablets, since Vitamin E and iron compounds are not the best of friends.

297

298

If you have chronically cold hands, bathe them regularly. Dip your hands and arms right up to the elbow joints in a tub of water at a temperature of 97 to 99 °F. After drying off, put on your clothes and exercise.

299

Essential oils made from cedar with lemon, rose geranium, lavender and pine are valuable assets for greasy hair. Apply three drops in half a pint of water to your hair every evening.

300

After you get up, go out into the snow and run on the spot for 5 to 10 minutes. Then dry yourself off quickly, moving your feet around in a circle, and put on your socks immediately.

301

During sleep, our cells renew themselves and waste products are eliminated. So it is no luxury to change the bed linen from time to time and wear fresh sleepwear every day. Sleeping naked is unhygienic because the substances eliminated through the skin get into the bed linen in this way.

302

If you have sleeping problems, you should check your bedroom for electrical smog. The bedroom is no place for radios and television sets; at the very least they should never be placed directly beside the bed. The same applies to alarm clocks connected to the mains power supply. You are better off with battery-operated devices.

303

Showering is quicker than taking a bath. And these days none of us think we have any time any more. Nevertheless, quite consciously allow yourself a bath now and then and do not let your pleasure be limited by the dictates of time. You should really make the most of a bath, enjoy its pleasant warmth and even occasionally close your eyes and listen to the depths of your soul.

304

This Taoist exercise will increase your mental vigour: stand up straight with relaxed knees. Bend your arms. Breathe out deeply while stretching your arms downwards. Now tense all the muscles in your neck, stomach and bottom and at the same time push through with your knees. Stop for a couple of seconds. You will immediately feel renewed energy.

Buy yourself a highly-concentrated firmness cocktail made from ivy, horsetail or sea collagen from the pharmacy. Rub it on your breasts and your neckline for low-cut clothes.

305

306

A proven remedy against pain and tension is a hot hayseed pad. It also stimulates the connective tissue.

307

Make yourself beautiful and fit with the power of the sea. Do not begrudge your skin a seawater exfoliation. Mix a cup of sea salt with three dessertspoons of jojoba oil and then apply it to the skin with circling movements.

308

After a shower, you should stimulate your skin. Tap all parts of your body systematically with your bare hand or with a massage brush.

309

You can afford to do this little exercise even in the office: stand squarely with your knees relaxed and roll from the tips of your toes to your heels and back again. Do this for about five minutes. Increase your speed at the same time.

310

Do not begrudge your legs and bottom a daily massage with lemon oil. Two drops of essential lemon oil are mixed with three dessertspoons of jojoba oil. Use this mixture for the massage.

311

Cinnamon tea gets your circulation going. Pour boiling water over a teaspoon of black tea and half a stick of cinnamon. Strain after five minutes – a fantastic remedy for exhaustion.

312

If you sit around for longish periods in the evenings, eat fatty food and drink rather more than usual, this can lead to a stomach and intestinal upset. Take an ounce each of cinnamon and clove powder and mix with lukewarm water. Drink a small spirit glass full of it three times a day.

Regardless of whether your meals are hot, spicy or sweet, get used to seasoning them more. Every now and then also get some exotic spices – they are excellent for your health.

313

You can help relieve facial tension by massaging with circling and slightly kneading movements from the side of your nose to your chin.

314

315

Put the fingertips of both hands on the side of the nape of your neck. With a circling motion of the thumbs, move upwards to the hairline of the skull. After five minutes you will feel the beneficial effect.

316

Buy your groceries with health in mind. Olives, for example. Most pickled olives do not contain living lactic acid bacteria. That is why you should in principle only buy olives loose in market halls or at weekly markets.

317

A gentle stomach massage that you can carry out yourself is helpful for stress or digestive complaints. Lie on your back with your legs slightly bent. With light pressure, move your hands in a clockwise, circular direction over the abdominal wall. It is important to massage with a continuous movement.

318

Sit on your heels. Bring your arms to shoulder height and place your fists against each other. Now breathe out. As you breathe in again, stretch one arm out to the side. As you do so, imagine that this hand is holding a rubber band and that you are fighting against this force. When your arm is completely outstretched and your lungs are full of air, open your hand and let go of the imaginary rubber band.

Take a moment to think about what you eat every day. To prevent illness you should eat fruit and vegetables at least five times a day. If you remember to do this regularly, it will soon become a matter of course. And vegetables taste good too!

319

320

Nuts are little bundles of energy. They contain vitamin B and E, mineral substances, trace elements and unsaturated fatty acids.

321

If you have ever been to Asia, you will know that people there rarely serve sweet dishes full of sugar and calories. Instead they eat fruity desserts or just delicious fruit.

322

Wintertime is flu season. Colds are more common in winter because people stay close together in enclosed spaces more often. So avoid such gatherings of people and wash your hands frequently.

Banish cloth handkerchiefs from your wardrobe once and for all! They are carriers of bacteria. Paper handkerchiefs should be thrown down the toilet after use: in the waste paper basket, the viruses could continue to spread.

323

324

Good sleep is a blessing. But you can rarely sleep well without a good mattress. Examine your old mattress critically some time and buy a new one if necessary. But make sure you get advice from a good specialist shop.

325

Even if it is cold outside, you should take a cold footbath every now and then. Put your feet in water at a temperature of about 50 °F for half a minute. Then dry your feet quickly.

Not only are alternating showers tremendously refreshing and can dispel tiredness, they also strengthen the resistance of the entire organism.

326

327

You should become accustomed to regularly going to the sauna. It purifies the body and strengthens its defences, especially against infectious diseases. However, it is important that you do this regularly. If you have circulatory and heart problems, you should consult your doctor beforehand; the same applies to people with varicose veins.

328

Almond oil and almond soap – obtainable from whole food and health food shops – are ideal for the care of dry and mature skin.

329

If you use a massage brush on your limbs, you should always brush towards the heart. The positive effect of such a massage can be seen in rosy-coloured skin with good blood circulation.

330

To stimulate the circulation, you can drink cinnamon tea. Simply pour hot water over a teaspoon of black tea with a quarter of a stick of cinnamon. Strain after five minutes.

331

Do not eat meat or sausage products too often. It is better to include fish in your diet more frequently.

332

Wash your whole body with a sponge from head to foot with cold water at a temperature of 60 °F. Do not dry yourself afterwards; simply lie down on your bed in your bathrobe.

333

With cool water (60 °F) shower your lower leg from the left outer side of the foot to the knee, then shower the right outer side downwards. Then it is the turn of the front and back of the calf.

334

Even if the sun is constantly hidden behind thick clouds in winter, you do not need to do without it. There can be few objections to occasionally getting moderate ray treatment at a reputable solar studio. Just do not overdo it!

335

Undertake to do simple yoga exercises over the next two days. Stand upright and place your hands against each other at chest height. Then breathe in and at the same time stretch your arms up, then behind. As you breathe out, bend far forward and down; in the process your fingertips should touch the ground.

A second yoga exercise:
lie down on the floor on your
stomach, bend your arms and
move your chest over the floor.
While doing this exercise, your
knees should be slightly bent.

336

337

If you want to cut back a bit on food but still feel like some cake, you should just compromise: choose a piece of fruit tart. The fruit contains vitamins and is healthy and the bit of sponge around it is not a serious nutritional sin.

338

If your nose is running, try to relieve your symptoms with a chamomile vapour bath. You just need a fairly large bowl – pour boiling water into it over a handful of chamomile flowers. Sit down in front of this bowl and cover your head with a towel. Such a treatment can of course be carried out more comfortably with an inhaler.

339

Night creams are richer in nutrients than day creams and can also be used in winter during the day. As they contain more oil, they protect you well against frost and cold.

340

If your skin has become red and chapped because of the cold, you can soothe it with a compress of chamomile or lavender. Honey dissolved in lukewarm water also has a pleasant effect on irritated skin.

341

Men have thicker skin than women and also believe that skin care is not a matter for them. How wrong can they be! Even men's skin needs care. Soap is not recommended; instead a mild cream soap that returns the oil to the skin should be used. After this, a cream should be applied that protects against the effects of cold weather.

342

If you have rough, dry and
chapped hands, wash them
as little as possible so that
no more oil and moisture are
removed from the skin.

Once a week in winter, you should treat your hands with a pack. Take three dessertspoons of jojoba oil and carefully rub it into your hands. Then envelop them in thin cotton gloves and leave on overnight.

343

344

If you wash your hair with a shampoo of your choice, you can still use your own power mixture as a conditioner. Mix an egg yolk with a teaspoon of fruit vinegar and add lukewarm water to it.

Here is a relaxation tip for in between times –
but only once your muscles are already warmed
up. Put both arms in front of your chest and clasp
your hands together. Now pull your arms apart.
Keep this resistance going for a few seconds.

345

Even if it is icy cold, go swimming regularly. But not in warm water – go swimming in a cold-water pool. Ten minutes will suffice at first, but increase your time over the next few days. As you do this, you will see how warm it will get for you.

346

347

Jogging is an excellent exercise, not only if the sun is shining. It is important to run regularly even if it is cold or drizzling. You just have to put on warm clothes or slip on some rain protection.

Sport – whatever type you choose –
is like a drug. During exercise, the
organism releases "happiness
hormones" that have a tremendously
beneficial effect on body and soul.

348

349

If you simply cannot get over your gloomy winter mood, it is high time to get out those cross-country skis. Cross-country skiing is an outstanding remedy for winter depression.

Buy yourself dried yarrow from the chemist's and make yourself a cup of tea with it. This drink is very effective against colds.

351

You do not have to put up with headaches. There can be no objection to taking some medicine. But do without preparations containing various mixed substances. It is better to take mono-preparations with the active ingredients acetylsalicylic acid, paracetamol or ibuprofen.

352

If in spite of this you do catch a cold and come down with a fever, avoid medicines that lower your temperature: fever is the most effective way of fighting the infection. Drink hot tea and put a compress around your leg. This is the best way of helping your body cope with the infection.

353

If you are sweating with a feverish cold,
you must replace the lost fluid. Drink
water or herbal teas such as elderflower tea
or rose hip tea. Salted chicken broth
is beneficial because it replaces the lost
mineral substances.

354

Soothing teas are recommended for sore throats. Gargle with sage tea. Hot lemon tea diluted with water is ideal. Do not sweeten it with sugar, but with a teaspoon of honey. You can also suck Iceland moss lozenges.

For inflamed tonsils, sucking ice cream also helps; in this way the tissue, hot from the inflammation, is cooled down. Eating ice-cream is not recommended if you have a cough. In this case, hot teas are better if you have a cold.

355

If you use essential oils as bath essences, make sure that they never come into contact with the skin, as they can be very aggressive and burn it. Store the oils in light-protected (dark) bottles.

356

If you want to do something for your grey matter, get yourself a ginkgo preparation. Such preparations protect the blood-brain barrier and improve its filtering and control function. This improves your memory and powers of concentration.

357

358

Eat three almonds a day – this sweet nut
drives away headaches and insomnia.

359

Add three dessertspoons of linseed to a pint of boiling water. Allow to draw for ten minutes and then strain. This tea is rich in vitamin F. You can also add linseed to any soup. In this way you supply your intestines with ideal roughage.

360

Thyme oil encourages the removal of mucus, alleviates cramps, soothes sore throats and disinfects the airways. Even if you have a cough, you can alleviate the unpleasant attacks. Although it is a natural remedy, you should not use excessive amounts of thyme oil.

361

From the point of view of quality, essential oils can vary greatly. You should only buy them from the chemist's, even if they are more expensive there. The pharmacist can give you advice and you can be sure that you are getting only the best quality.

362

The eye needs a lot of light, at least 300 lux, for reading. So make sure that your study has enough artificial light during the dark season.

363

Here's a way to toughen yourself up
in winter: if there is snow outside, simply
take a handful and rub it on your face.

Lactic pickled vegetables are bliss for the stomach
and intestines; do not let a day go by without eating pickles.
The Japanese include them in practically every meal.

364

365

Homeopathic medicines work gently against colds. Aconitum is effective for symptoms that go hand in hand with fever. Allium cepa is effective against head colds and apois mellefica wards off coughs and sore throats. Belladonna is taken for fever.